THE LIFE SCIENCE LIBRARY™

Animal Adaptations
for Survival

Elizabeth Rose

The Rosen Publishing Group's

PowerKids Press™

New York

For Flannery Emma and Emma Bean

Published in 2006 by The Rosen Publishing Group, Inc.
29 East 21st Street, New York, NY 10010

First Edition

Editor: Rachel O'Connor
Book Design: Albert B. Hanner

Photo Credits: Cover, title page, pp. 10, 15 (bottom right), 19 (top) © Digital Vision; pp. 4, 9 (top and bottom), 12, 13 (top), 17 (top), 21 (bottom right), 22 © Digital Stock; p. 5 (top) © Perry Conway/Corbis, p. 5 (bottom) © James De Bounevialle; Cordaiy Photo Library Ltd./Corbis; p. 7 (top) © Martin B. Winters; Frank Lane Picture Agency/Corbis, p. 7 (bottom) © Roger Tidman/Corbis; p. 11 (top) © Tim Lamen/National Geographic/Getty Images; p. 11 (bottom) © Chris Taylor; Cordaiy Photo Library Ltd./Corbis; p. 13 (bottom) © Jim Richardson/Corbis; p.15 (top) © Joe McDonald/Corbis, p. 15 (bottom left) © Chris Mattison; Frank Lane Picture Agency/Corbis; p. 17 (bottom) © Brand X Pictures/Getty Images; p. 18 © Brian J. Skerry/National Geographic/Getty Images; p. 19 (bottom) © Charles Mauzy/Corbis; p. 21 (top) © Ralph A. Clevenger/Corbis; p. 21 (bottom left) © Richard Nowitz/National Geographic/Getty Images.

Library of Congress Cataloging-in-Publication Data

Rose, Elizabeth, 1970–
Animal adaptations for survival/ Elizabeth Rose.
     p. cm. — (The life science library)
Includes bibliographical references (p.   ).
ISBN 1-4042-2817-9 (lib. bdg.)
1. Animals—Adaptation—Juvenile literature. [1. Animals—Adaptation.] I. Title. II. Life science library (New York, N.Y.)
QL49 .R63 2005
591.4—dc22

                              2003023177
                              Rev.

Manufactured in the United States of America

Contents

1 Adapting to the World   4

2 Changing over Time   6

3 Getting Around   8

4 Staying Safe   10

5 Hiding in Plain Sight   12

6 Mimics and Imitators   14

7 Hunting   16

8 Building a Home   18

9 Adapting to Heat and Cold   20

10 Living in Groups   22

   Glossary   23

   Index   24

   Web Sites   24

Adapting to the World

Seals have adapted over time so that they have flippers. This adaptation means that although seals are not great walkers on land, they are graceful and fast in the water.

What do animals need to **survive**? Like humans, animals need shelter, food, a way to get around, and protection from things that cause them harm. Unlike humans, animals do not have supermarkets, cars, or apartments. Instead animals' bodies and **behaviors** are specially suited to their needs and where they live, or their environment. Special features that help animals survive are called **physical adaptations**. Behaviors that help animals survive are called behavioral adaptations. Most animals **develop** adaptations over long periods of time. This process of change is called **evolution**.

Skunks have adapted to protect themselves by spraying a stinky liquid from under their tails. As many unhappy dogs discover, the skunk can squirt its liquid more than 9 feet (2.7 m) away.

Moles have large paws that are shaped like shovels, which make them very good diggers. Moles also stay in their holes most of the time. This behavioral adaptation of staying underground helps keep a mole safe from predators.

Changing over Time

Evolution works by a process called natural selection. This means that the animals that can adapt to the environment tend to survive. Animals that cannot adapt die out over time. The peppered moth is a good example. This moth used to be pale colored to **blend** in with the pale tree trunks where it lived. This helped the moth hide from things that might want to eat it. When pollution in the air darkened the trunks, however, the pale-colored moths could no longer blend in and hide. The pale moths were eaten by birds. By chance some peppered moths were born darker. In the past these darker moths would have been eaten first. However, they blended in with the dark trunks and survived. Almost all the peppered moths are now dark colored.

Evolution is usually a very slow process, and changes in a population can take many centuries. Moths, however, have very short life spans, so scientists were able to see natural selection at work on evolution over the course of just a few years. Here we see the light-colored peppered moth (above) and the darker moth (below). Over time the population of moths changed until almost all the moths were dark colored.

Getting Around

To survive, animals must be able to get around. Movement lets animals hunt for food and escape from danger. Different animals have adapted their movements to suit their environments in wonderful ways. Cheetahs use their legs to run up to 60 miles per hour (97 km/h) to catch **prey**. Most of the insects, bats, and the 9,000 kinds of birds in the world use wings to get around. Penguins, however, do not use their wings to fly. Their wings have adapted to work like fins so that they can swim underwater. Often animals must move to find more food. When winter comes some animals move to warmer places to avoid the cold and to find food during the winter. This behavioral adaptation is called **migration**.

Migration is a behavioral adaptation. Some animals, such as the wildebeest pictured here, migrate to find more food when their food source is used up during winter.

The cheetah hunts either alone or in small groups. Seeking its prey out in the morning or late in the afternoon, the cheetah quietly stalks its prey before breaking into a fast run. This method of hunting is suited to its habitat, which is open grassland. The cheetah is the fastest of all cats and is the only animal capable of running down black bucks and gazelles. The cheetah usually measures around 55 inches (140 cm) long and weighs up to 130 pounds (59 kg).

Staying Safe

The poison dart frog uses poison as its adaptation for protection. Most of the 170 species of this frog are poisonous. In the most poisonous species, one drop of poison can kill an adult human being. The bright color of the poison dart frogs warns predators that the frogs are poisonous.

Animals have adapted to stay safe where they live. Spines, shells, and claws are all examples of physical adaptations that help animals stay safe. For example, hedgehogs are covered in sharp, 1-inch- (2.5 cm) long spines that protect them from animals that want to eat them. Cats have claws for protection. Animals also have behavioral adaptations that keep them safe. When a hedgehog feels in danger, it rolls itself into a tight ball to protect its soft belly and nose. A cat may run up a tree when it is chased. These physical and behavioral adaptations have been programmed into these animals over many generations.

Many kinds of turtles have hard shells that make it very hard for predators to attack them. When a turtle senses danger, it may pull its head and legs into its shell. The turtle has another slightly softer shell covering its belly. Because of this shell, a predator will not be able to bite into the turtle, even if the turtle has been flipped over.

Very few predators will approach the hedgehog when it is rolled into a spiny ball!

Hiding in Plain Sight

In the summer the snowshoe hare's fur is brown. This is so the hare can blend in with the dry summer grass and leaves. In the winter, however, its coat changes color and becomes pure white. The hare can then blend in with the snow!

Some animals have developed **camouflage** that blends in with their environment. Camouflage is a physical adaptation. It can hide an animal from a hungry **predator**, but it is not the same as hiding. Rabbits that run into underground dens when they hear foxes are hiding. When rabbits use camouflage, on the other hand, they hold still against backgrounds that match their fur. The matching background and fur make the rabbit hard to see. This adaptation helps the rabbit escape the notice of predators. Baby animals often have their own special camouflage. For example, the harp seal is born pure white to blend in with snow.

Stripes on zebras might not look like good camouflage, but they are! The stripes break up the shape of the animal's body, making it hard for other animals to recognize it as an animal at all. In fact a hunting lion looking at a pack of striped zebras may not even be able to tell one animal from another. The lion's eyes are tricked by all the stripes!

A baby deer, or fawn, is not strong enough to walk very far. To stay safe while they are lying on the forest floor, fawns are spotted brown and white to camouflage themselves. When fawns grow up, they lose their baby camouflage and become solid brown.

Mimics and Imitators

Animals can also use camouflage by pretending to be the leaf or branch on which they are hiding. This kind of behavior is called **imitation**. Chameleons are well-known imitators. Their color matches the place where they live, which is usually among the leaves of a tree. Their flat, oval bodies are leaf shaped. Some chameleons grow spiky crests on their backs that blend with the edges of leaves. Some animals protect themselves by being mimics, or copycats. For example, the coral snake, which has bright red and black markings, is very poisonous. The harmless king snake mimics, or copies, this snake by having the same markings. In this way the king snake is more likely to be left alone by predators.

A king snake's pattern mimics that of a coral snake. Because the king snake looks like the very poisonous coral snake, predators are likely to leave the king snake alone.

The harmless hoverfly mimics the wasp's markings. Predators, thinking the fly is a wasp and can sting, leave the hoverfly alone.

Chameleons' skin matches the green leaves on which they live. Many people think that chameleons change color to match their background. Chameleons actually change their colors to communicate, or share feelings, with other chameleons. For example, if a chameleon is angry or scared, it will change color.

Hunting

Predators have also developed camouflage and behaviors that help them hunt for food. The polar bear's white coat blends in with the frozen landscape of the north. This helps hide the bear from the animals, such as seals, for which it hunts. Tigers' stripes help them blend in with the tall grass in which they hunt. The stripes also break up the shape of the tiger, making it hard for prey to spot the cat when it is standing still. Most predators also need to be fast and strong to hunt and catch the animals they eat. They often have sharp claws, beaks, and teeth. Owls are very well adapted for hunting. They have strong wings with special feathers to help them fly silently, and huge eyes for seeing in the dark.

Great white sharks have sharp teeth that are curved backward to hold squirming fish. When the front teeth begin to get dull, they simply fall out. They are replaced by new sharp teeth that have been growing in a row behind the old teeth.

As you can see from this photograph, almost every part of the owl is made for hunting! Owls also hunt at night, when the animals they eat, such as mice, are most active. Hunting at night is a behavioral adaptation that helps the owl get the food it needs.

Supersensitive ears

Large eyes to see in the dark

Hooked beak for ripping and tearing

Special feathers that allow the owl to fly silently

Sharp talons for snatching prey

Building a Home

The hermit crab has a special behavior that keeps it sheltered. A hermit crab is born without a shell. This crab's adaptive behavior is to move into an empty shell. The crab lives there until it grows too big to fit in its borrowed home. Then the crab moves out and finds a bigger shell!

Animals, like people, need shelter to keep them dry and warm in cold climates and cool and protected from sunlight in hot ones. Different animals have different adaptations that allow them to make their homes. Some dig or build homes. Animals such as spiders spin homes. Beavers are the most famous builders of the animal world. They use their enormous front teeth to chop down trees. Then they use their strong, flat tails to swim. While swimming they carry large branches and tree trunks. They use these to build their homes, called lodges. The hermit crab, which is born without a shell, finds empty shells in which to live.

A spiderweb is made of fine silken threads. Spiders first spun silk so that they could protect their eggs and so that they could line the nests of their young. Later most used this silk to weave a web and trap their prey. In this photograph you can see that the spider has successfully caught a bug in a silky web.

Beaver lodges are so well built that generations of a beaver family will use the same lodge for hundreds of years. Beavers' lodges always have underwater entrances to keep out uninvited guests. To make sure the entrance stays underwater, beavers build strong dams downstream from the lodges. These dams create a calm, deep pool in which the beavers can swim. To build underwater, beavers can hold their breath for up to 15 minutes!

Adapting to Heat and Cold

   During winter, animals have three choices. They can sleep through the cold season, they can migrate to warmer places, or they can adapt to the cold. Some animals, such as bears, sleep for long periods and wake from time to time. Some animals sleep right through the winter. This kind of deep sleep is called **hibernation**. A hibernating animal, such as a hedgehog, slows down its heartbeat to about one beat per minute and may only breathe once every half hour! If an animal lives in an area where it is always cold, then it needs to adapt to the cold. Most **mammals** who live in cold areas do this by growing two layers of hair to keep them warm. For example, arctic foxes and arctic hares have double coats.

Bears deal with cold weather by sleeping for most of the winter. They still wake up occasionally when the weather heats up or if they hear a noise.

Some hot-weather animals, such as this camel, can go for days without water. The camel's hump stores watery fat that the camel's body can use when no water is available.

Many animals that live in hot weather, such as African elephants, have big ears. Their big ears help them stay cool because they lose their body heat through their ears. Elephants also have very thick skin that keeps them from losing too much water.

Living in Groups

Some predators live in groups, too. Lions live in groups made up of 4 to 12 related females, their babies, and 1 to 6 males. These groups, called prides, travel together and share food that the female lions, or lionesses, have caught.

Many animals protect themselves by living in groups. This adaptation can protect animals from predators. Antelopes, for example, travel in giant herds across Africa's grasslands. Predators will only attack antelopes that become separated from the herd.

Sometimes animals have to adapt to living in crowds of people! This can mean big problems for most animals. Some animals, such as rats, mice, and even raccoons, have adapted to sharing space with humans. Adaptations are remarkable. Because of adaptations, each and every animal fits exactly into its own environment.

22

Glossary

adaptations (a-dap-TAY-shunz) Changes in an animal that help it stay alive.

behaviors (bee-HAY-vyurz) Ways to act.

blend (BLEND) To mix together completely.

camouflage (KA-muh-flaj) A color or a pattern that matches the surroundings and helps hide something.

develop (dih-VEH-lup) To grow.

evolution (eh-vuh-LOO-shun) Change that happens over many years.

hibernation (hy-bur-NAY-shun) To spend the winter in a sleeplike state, with heart rate and breathing rate slowed down.

imitation (ih-muh-TAY-shun) To copy someone or something.

mammals (MA-mulz) Warm-blooded animals that have hair and backbones, breathe air, and feed milk to their young.

migration (my-GRAY-shun) Movement from one place to another.

physical (FIH-zih-kul) Having to do with the body.

predator (PREH-duh-ter) An animal that kills other animals for food.

prey (PRAY) An animal that is hunted by another animal for food.

survive (sur-VYV) To continue to exist.

Index

A
adaptations,
   behavioral, 4,
   10
adaptations,
   physical, 4, 10,
   12

C
camouflage, 12,
   14, 16

E
environment, 4, 8,
   12, 22

evolution, 4, 6

H
herds, 22
hibernation, 20

I
imitation, 14

M
mammals, 20
migration, 8, 20
mimics, 14
moth, peppered, 6

N
natural selection, 6

P
predator, 12, 16,
   22
prey, 8, 16

S
shelter, 4, 18

Web Sites

Due to the changing nature of Internet links, PowerKids Press has developed an online list of Web sites related to the subject of this book. This site is updated regularly. Please use this link to access the list:
www.powerkidslinks.com/lsl/adaptbeh/